LEARNING ABOUT
JESU

Lois Rock

Illustrated by Maureen Galvani

LION
Children's Books

Text by Lois Rock
Illustrations copyright © 2002 Maureen Galvani
This edition copyright © 2002 Lion Publishing

The moral rights of the author and illustrator
have been asserted

Published by
Lion Publishing plc
Mayfield House, 256 Banbury Road,
Oxford OX2 7DH, England
www.lion-publishing.co.uk
ISBN 0 7459 4733 6

First edition 2002
1 3 5 7 9 10 8 6 4 2 0

A catalogue record for this book is available
from the British Library

Typeset in 16/26 Carmina Light BT
Printed and bound in Singapore

Introduction: Who is Jesus?

Jesus is the name of the one whom Christians follow. He is often called Jesus Christ.

He lived a very long time ago, but people still know a lot about him.

His story is told in books called the Gospels: the Gospel of Matthew, the Gospel of Mark, the Gospel of Luke and the Gospel of John. They are now a part of the Christian Bible. They were all written just after the time of Jesus and include stories told by Jesus' own special friends.

This book tells you some of the most important things that Christians believe about Jesus.

1 When did Jesus live?

Jesus lived about 2,000 years ago.

When he was born, only a few people took any notice. Yet the things Jesus said and did have made him very famous.

After Jesus died, the news about him spread. More and more people began to follow his teaching. Many years later, Christians decided to number the years from the one in which they thought Jesus was born.

That same way of counting the years is still used in many places.

For 2,000 years there have been people who have lived as followers of Jesus – as Christians.

2 Who were Jesus' parents?

Jesus' mother was called Mary.

Luke's book about Jesus says she was a young woman who lived in the town of Nazareth, in the region of Galilee. She was planning to get married to a man named Joseph.

One day, an angel came. The angel told Mary that God had chosen her to have a child; he would be known as the Son of God.

Mary was very puzzled, but the angel said that God could make anything happen.

Later, an angel spoke to Joseph as he lay dreaming. The angel told Joseph to marry Mary and look after her and the child. Joseph agreed.

The Land of Jesus

Sea of Galilee

Nazareth

River Jordan

Jerusalem

Bethlehem

Dead Sea

Christians believe that Jesus, the son of Mary, is also the Son of God.

3 When was Jesus' birthday?

No one made a special note of the date when Jesus was born, but there are stories about what happened.

Luke's story says that Mary and Joseph went on a journey to the town of Bethlehem. The town was crowded, and Mary and Joseph had to shelter in a stable. Jesus was born there.

Out on the hillsides were shepherds. Angels came and told them about the baby. The shepherds went to see.

Matthew's story says that wise men came from far away to Bethlehem. They were following a star. 'It will lead us to a king,' they said. It led them to Jesus. They gave him rich gifts: gold, frankincense and myrrh.

 Christians remember the birth of Jesus at Christmas.

4 Did Jesus do special things from the time he was a baby?

The stories about Jesus' birth say that he was special from the beginning, but as a boy his life was ordinary.

Boys in Jesus' day went to school to learn about their God.

They also learned a trade from their father.

When Jesus was grown up, he became a preacher and a teacher. The people in his home town were surprised: was it right for an ordinary young man to do that? The surprises were only just beginning!

Christians believe that Jesus was human just like everyone, even though he was also God's Son.

5 Was Jesus' teaching special?

Jesus said he had good news to tell people. It was about something called the kingdom of God.

Jesus told people the way to live in order to be part of the kingdom: 'Love your enemies.'

'Forgive others the wrong they do to you.'

'Do for others what
you want them to do
for you.'

Christians believe that Jesus helped people find
the good and right way to live.

6 Did Jesus do magic things?

As Jesus went about preaching and teaching, he also worked miracles: he calmed a storm by speaking; he turned water into wine; with a touch, he made sick people well.

Some people were happy and excited, but others were worried. Did Jesus have good power or bad power?

One day, Jesus healed a blind person who had never been able to see before.

People asked him what he thought had happened.

He said this: 'Jesus cured me of my blindness... Unless this man came from God, he would not be able to do a thing.'

 Christians believe that Jesus had God's power to heal people.

7 Did people like Jesus?

Many people liked Jesus. Some became his followers.

He chose twelve special friends, the disciples.

There were hundreds of others who loved to listen to him and followed him everywhere. Jesus welcomed everyone – even the kinds of people that others look down on.

He told a story to help people understand why:

'Once there was a shepherd who had a hundred sheep. One day, he counted the flock and found there were only ninety-nine.

'He left the ninety-nine in the pasture and went to find the lost sheep. He carried it home safely. Then he asked his friends to come and celebrate.'

Jesus explained that God cares for each and every person and does not want anyone to feel lost or alone.

Christians believe that Jesus helped people understand more about God's love and forgiveness.

8 Did anyone not like Jesus?

Some people who knew Jesus did not like him at all.

Many of the religious teachers and priests did not like him.

They did not believe that Jesus was teaching people the right thing.

They didn't think he kept all the rules and traditions carefully enough.

There was another problem too. Jesus' people believed that God had promised to send them a special king – the Christ. Some of them were beginning to think that Jesus was the Christ.

If Jesus started acting like a king, that would upset the government. Then there would be all kinds of fighting and trouble.

The teachers and the priests decided they would have to get rid of him.

Christians believe that Jesus was the Christ: not a king who caused fighting, but the King of love and peace.

9 What happened to Jesus in the end?

The people who did not like Jesus kept looking for a way to get rid of him.

In the end, one of Jesus' disciples, Judas Iscariot, told the priests where they could find Jesus when he was alone.

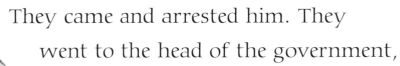

They came and arrested him. They went to the head of the government, Pontius Pilate, and asked to have Jesus put to death. Jesus was nailed to a cross of wood and hung up to die.

Jesus did not fight back. From the cross, he said a prayer: 'Father, forgive them. They don't know what they are doing.'

Christians believe that Jesus died on the cross and forgave the very worst things that people can do.

10 Where was Jesus buried?

One of Jesus' followers was a wealthy man named Joseph. He asked Pilate if he could take Jesus' body and bury it.

He had it laid in a tomb rather like a cave and had the stone door rolled shut.

The next day was the sabbath day of rest. The day after that, some women went back to the tomb. They were frightened when they saw that the door was open and the body was gone.

Then one of them saw Jesus. The disciples saw Jesus. Other friends said they had seen Jesus. Soon, Jesus' close followers were all sure he was alive again.

Christians believe that Jesus rose from death, and that God's love is stronger than death.

11 Where is Jesus now?

Jesus' friends saw him many times, for forty days.

He told them to spread the good news of God's kingdom to all the world.

Jesus' friends saw him go.

Then they remembered what he had told them before: 'Now I am going to heaven to prepare a place for you.'

With help from God, they began to tell the news.

The news has spread all round the world.

Christians still tell the story of Jesus. Every day, people listen to the message of love and forgiveness and a welcome in heaven.

12 Do Jesus' followers feel lonely without him?

Just before Jesus died, he shared one last meal with his friends.

As he shared the bread and wine with them, he told them always to share bread and wine together and to remember him.

He told them to love and help one another, and it would be as if they were loving and helping him.

Christians believe that Jesus is with them as they share bread and wine together, and as they love and help other people.

Who is Jesus?

1 For 2,000 years there have been people who have lived as followers of Jesus – as Christians.

2 Christians believe that Jesus, the son of Mary, is also the Son of God.

3 Christians remember the birth of Jesus at Christmas.

4 Christians believe that Jesus was human just like everyone, even though he was also God's Son.

5 Christians believe that Jesus helped people find the good and right way to live.

6 Christians believe that Jesus had God's power to heal people.

7 Christians believe that Jesus helped people understand more about God's love and forgiveness.

8 Christians believe that Jesus was the Christ: not a King who caused fighting, but the King of love and peace.

9 Christians believe that Jesus died on the cross and forgave the very worst things that people can do.

10 Christians believe that Jesus rose from death, and that God's love is stronger than death.

11 Christians still tell the story of Jesus. Every day, people listen to the message of love and forgiveness and a welcome in heaven.

12 Christians believe that Jesus is with them as they share bread and wine together, and as they love and help other people.